THUNDERSTORMS IN MY BRAIN

A SERVICE DOG STORY

WRITTEN BY ROSALIE BROWN
ILLUSTRATED BY ERIN VETTER

AuthorHouse™
1663 Liberty Drive
Bloomington, IN 47403
www.authorhouse.com
Phone: 1 (800) 839-8640

Published by AuthorHouse 08/07/2018

ISBN: 978-1-5462-5462-1 (sc)
ISBN: 978-1-5462-5464-5 (hc)
ISBN: 978-1-5462-5463-8 (e)

Library of Congress Control Number: 2018909230

Print information available on the last page.

authorHOUSE®

This book is dedicated to my friends, family, and teachers who have supported me and helped me to grow. To Canine Assistants, who gave me Rolex. And to every child with a disability or an illness. You are incredible.

On the last day of April, a baby was born, Rosalie.
Along with Laura and Megan, they were a set of three.

They were different, but inseparable, the best of friends.
They would always share that loving bond until the very end.

Then, on an overcast spring day, during a seasonal rain,
A thunderstorm also erupted inside Rosalie's brain.

The power to her body went out, and she fell to the ground.
Her body moved strangely, and she made some weird sounds.

Four minutes later she woke up inconsolably crying.
Her head hurt her so much that she thought she was dying.

Later, the doctors told her she was very sick; she was ill.
She had epilepsy, seizures, and now she had to take pills.

And the medicine stopped the seizures for the next several years.
Rosalie felt just like her sisters, friends, and peers.

She was incredibly happy because inside of her brain,
The thunderstorms had stopped; the sun came out, no more rain!

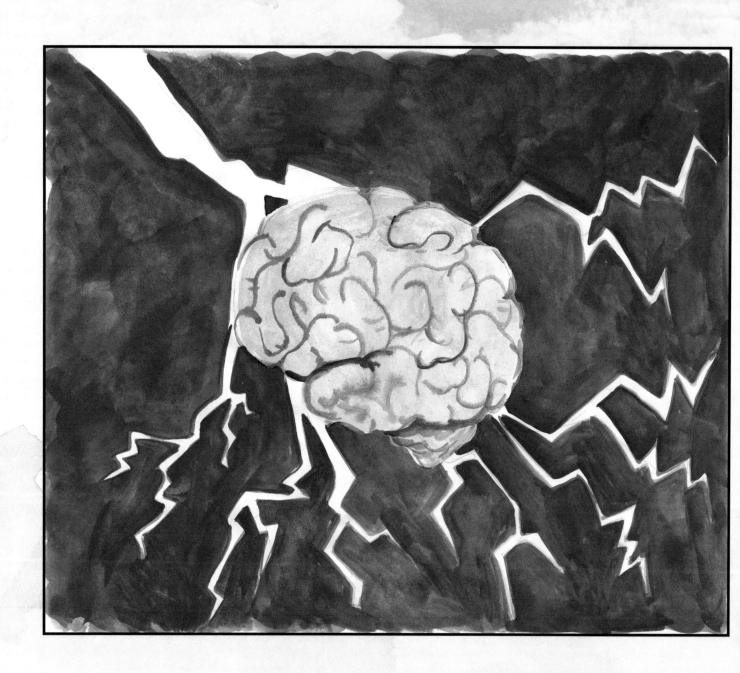

But as she got older, lightning struck once again in her mind.
She had more seizures than ever and many different kinds.

Her eyes would roll back; her face twitched, and her body would jerk,
And for seconds at a time her brain just stopped, wouldn't work.

School got so much harder as she couldn't remember what was said.
All Rosalie wanted to do was stay home and hide in her bed.

And as she got worse, and the number of seizures grew and grew,
Rosalie became scared, and her sisters and parents did too.

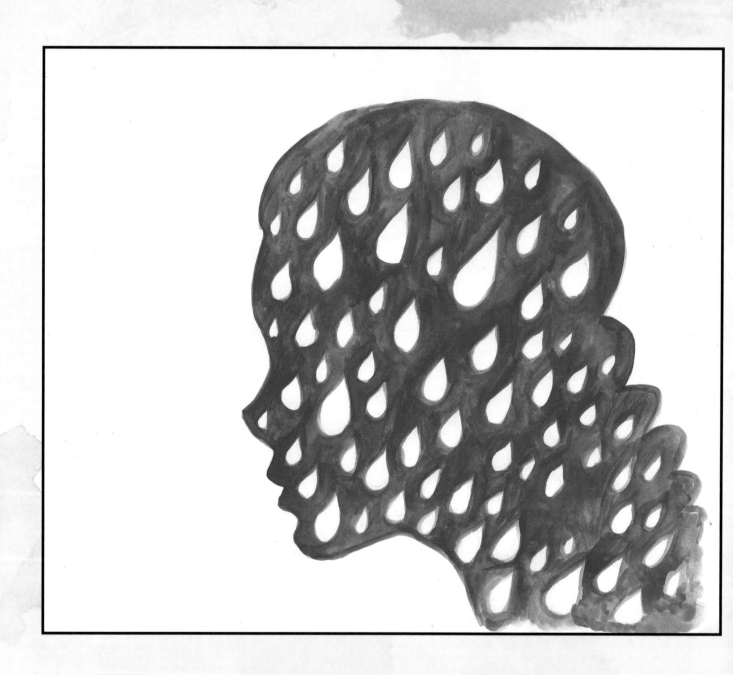

And because the thunderstorms and lightning would not go away,
In her brain it was dark and cloudy on happy, sunny days.

Soon it was time for college, so her sisters left and were gone.
Rosalie tried too, for two years, until she just couldn't go on.

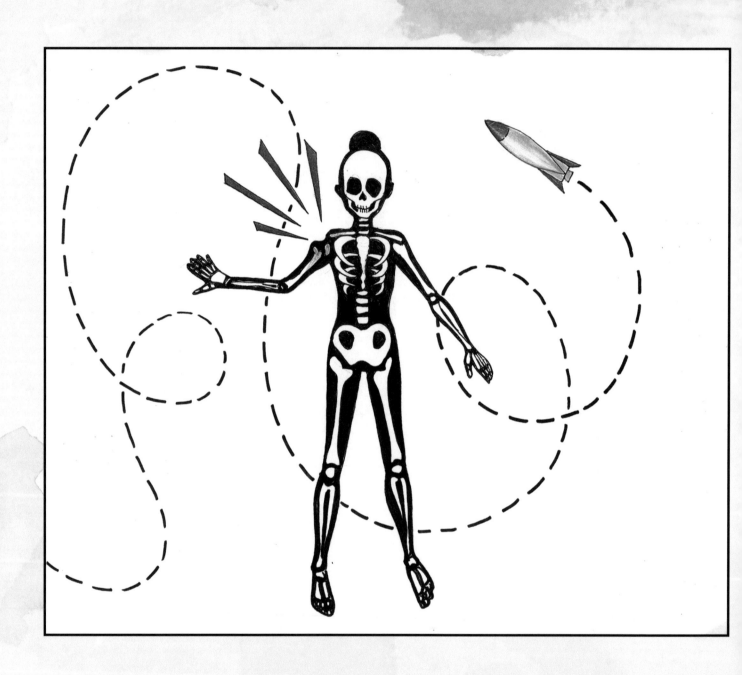

Her shoulder started dislocating, wouldn't stay in its socket.
She'd wake up from a big seizure feeling hit by a rocket.

At 300 seizures per day, life was dark, tiring, and rough.
It was scary and painful, and Rosalie just had enough!

She wondered why in the world God had created her at all,
If throughout her short life she would only continue to fall.

But on a beautiful happy farm, not an hour's drive away,
A special puppy was born on New Year's Eve day.

He was a cute Golden Retriever, a good service dog breed.
And he was born for a reason, to help a person in need.

For the next two years the puppy, Rolex, would train very hard.
Until he received his very own special person to guard.

His trainers took him on outings, and he had a lot of fun.
But he knew he couldn't help others until his training was done.

Finally, his trainers tried to match Rolex with a person to protect,
But he knew they weren't right because they couldn't connect.

Then on the farm, six months later, a trainer opened the door.
Rolex looked around the room sniffing, his leash sweeping the floor.

Waiting to meet her seizure response dog, there sat Rosalie.
Rolex knew instantly this was who his person would be.

He worked hard to help her, and Rosalie started to improve.
And life started to become not quite so dark, gloomy, and blue.

Her daily seizures came down from 300 to 50 that year.
Rolex had given her the chance to live her life without fear.

Thunderstorms still managed at times to rage in Rosalie's brain,
But Rosalie's life had started to turn towards normal again.

And through her dog's eyes she was able to catch a glimpse of God's plan.
Her seizures would no longer stop her; she started thinking, "I can."

She started loving herself, found a job, and doctors fixed her bad joints.
She found a partner, better medicine, and realized one point:

Her struggle was worth it if she could help others persevere.
She could show them the light at the end of the tunnel was near.

Disabilities like seizures are a great burden to bear,
But it's not unmanageable with other's support, love, and care.

And still there are thunderstorms striking inside Rosalie's brain,
But now rainbows and sunshine come more often than rain.

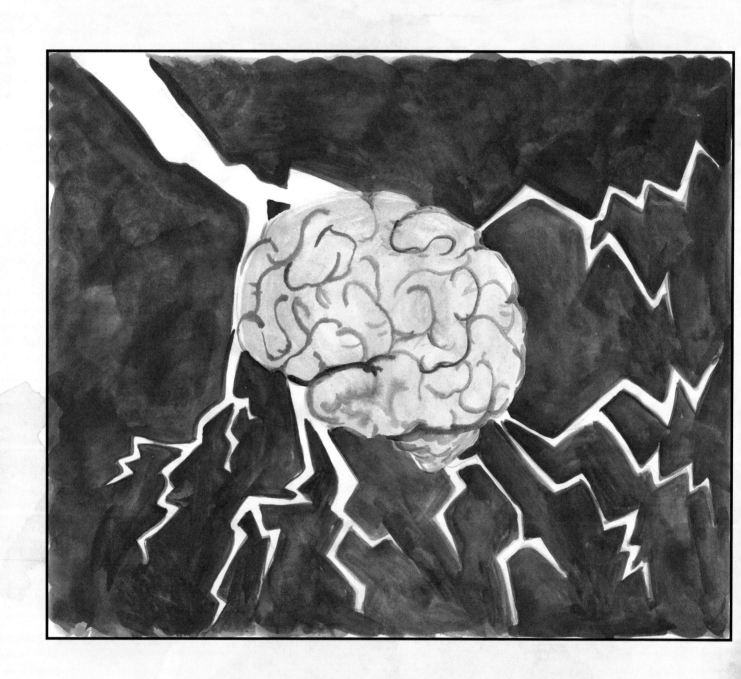

Printed in the United States
By Bookmasters